West Side Story

BASED ON A CONCEPTION OF JEROME ROBBINS

BOOK BY

ARTHUR LAURENTS

MUSIC BY

LEONARD BERNSTEIN

LYRICS BY

STEPHEN SONDHEIM

ENTIRE ORIGINAL PRODUCTION
DIRECTED AND CHOREOGRAPHED BY

JEROME ROBBINS

Simplified Piano Arrangements by
William Stickles

LEONARD BERNSTEIN Music Publishing Company LLC

T0070487

Tonight

Lyric by
Stephen Sondheim

Music by
Leonard Bernstein

Moderate Beguine tempo

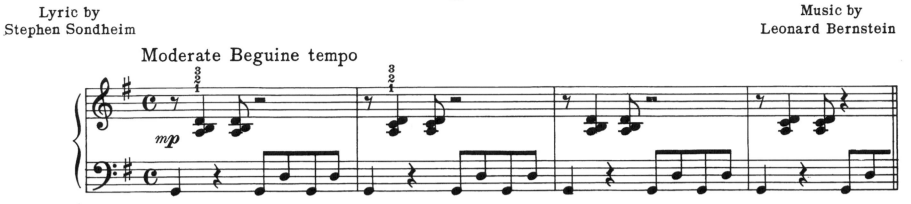

PAB - 613

Printed in U.S.A.

star. _____ To - night, to - night, I'll

see my love to - night. And for us, stars will

stop where they are! _____ To - day, the

min - utes seem like hours, ____ The hours ____ go so

slow - ly And still the sky is light._____ O

moon, grow bright, And make this end - less day, end - less

night,_____ to_____ night! To -

night!

Maria

Lyric by
Stephen Sondheim

Music by
Leonard Bernstein

PAB - 613

Printed in U.S.A.

sud-den-ly I've found how won-der-ful a sound can be! Ma - ri - a!___ Say it

loud and there's mu - sic play-ing, Say it soft and it's al-most like pray-ing.___ Ma -

ri - a,___ I'll nev - er stop say - ing, "Ma - ri - a."___

I Feel Pretty

Lyric by
Stephen Sondheim

Music by
Leonard Bernstein

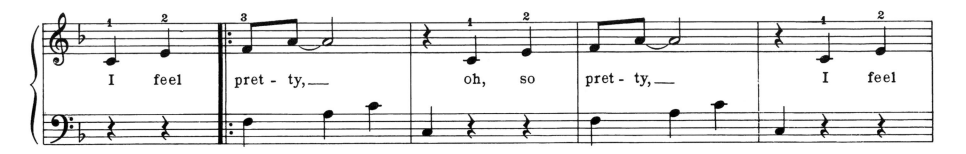

Printed in U.S.A.

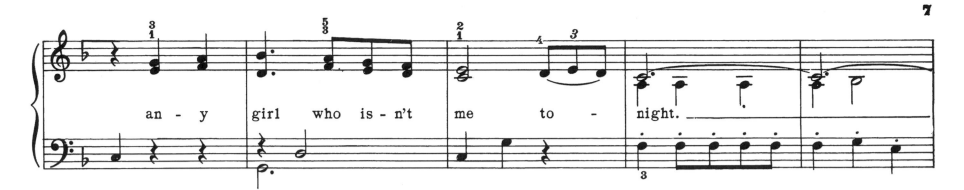

an - y girl who is - n't me to - night.

I feel charm-ing,— oh, so charm-ing,—

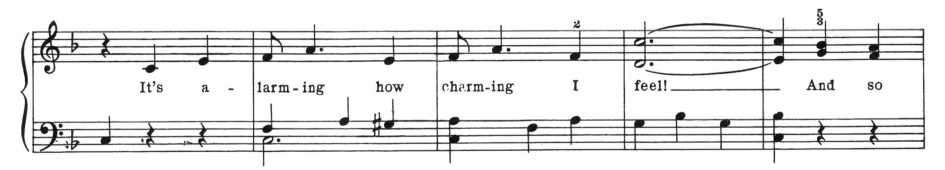

It's a - larm-ing how charm-ing I feel!_____ And so

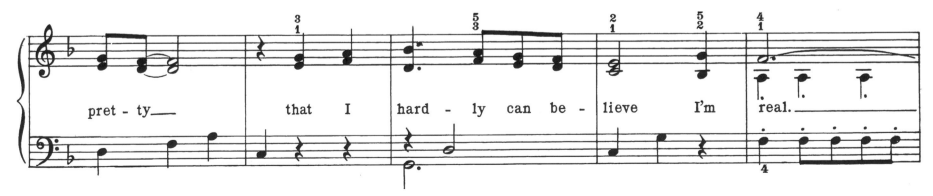

pret - ty___ that I hard - ly can be - lieve I'm real._____

See the pret - ty girl in that

mir - ror there. _____ Who can that at - trac - tive girl

be? _____ Such a pret - ty face, such a pret - ty

dress, such a pret - ty smile, such a pret - ty me! _____

I feel stun-ning,— and en-tranc-ing,—

Feel like run-ning and danc-ing for joy,——— For I'm

loved ——— by a pret-ty——— won-der-ful boy!———

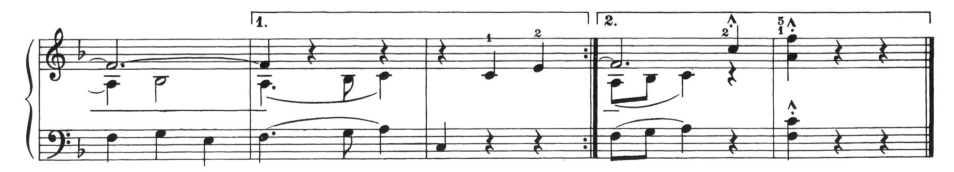

One Hand, One Heart

Lyric by
Stephen Sondheim

Music by
Leonard Bernstein

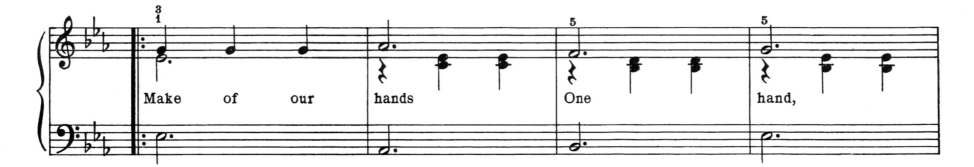

Printed in U.S.A.

vows one last vow; On - ly death will

part _____ us now. _____ Make of our

lives one life. Day af - ter day

one life. Now it be - gins, Now we

start;　One　hand,　one　heart.

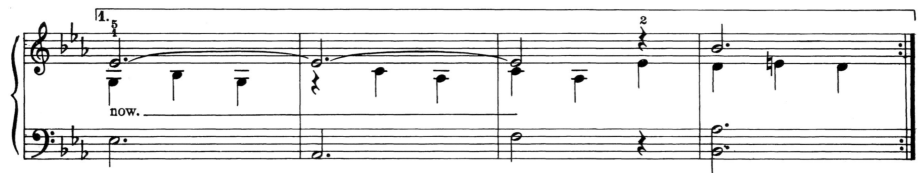

Ev - en　death　won't　part _____ us

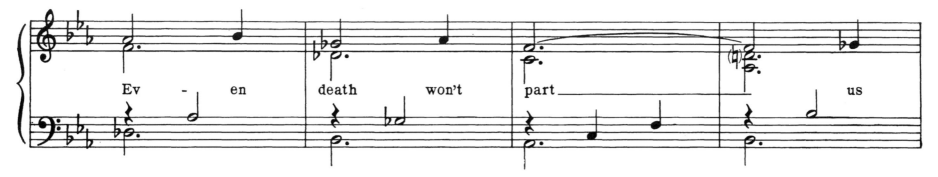

now. _____

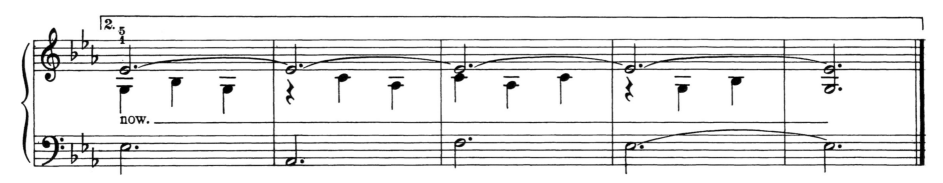

now. _____

America

Lyric by
Stephen Sondheim

Music by
Leonard Bernstein

Refrain

Brightly

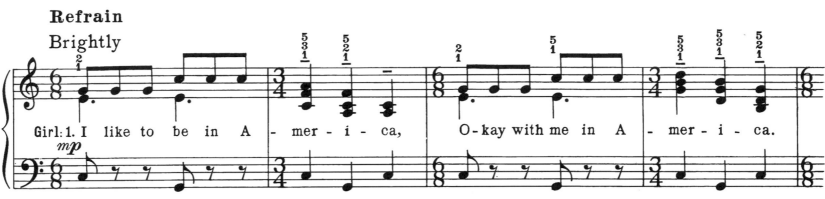

Girl: 1. I like to be in A - mer - i - ca, O-kay with me in A - mer - i - ca.

Ev-'ry-thing free in A - mer - i - ca, For a small fee in A - mer - i - ca!

To next strain | For 5th verse | *Fine*

PAB - 613

Printed in U.S.A.

Verse

Girl: 1. I like the cit - y of San Juan.— Boy: I know a boat you can

get on.— Girl: Hun - dreds of flow - ers in

full bloom. Boy: Hun - dreds of peo - ple in each room!

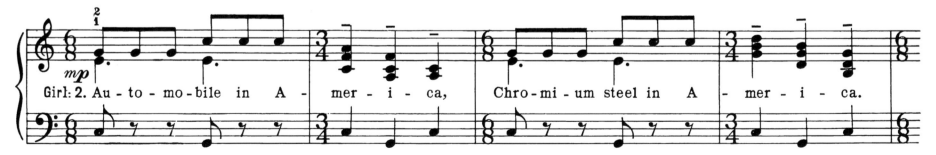

Girl: 2. Au - to - mo - bile in A - mer - i - ca, Chro - mi - um steel in A - mer - i - ca.

* An octave higher (ad lib).

Wi - re spoke wheel in A - mer - i - ca, Ver - y big deal in A - mer - i - ca!

Girl: 2. I'll drive a Bu - ick through San Juan._ Boy: If there's a road you can

drive on._ Girl: I'll give my cous - ins a

*An octave higher (ad lib).

D. C.

free ride._ Boy: How you fit all of them in - side?_

Refrain 3
Both: Immigrant goes to America,
      Many hellos in America.
      Nobody knows in America
      Puerto Rico's in America!

Verse 3
Girl: When I will go back to San Juan,
Boy: When you will shut up and be gone?
Girl: I'll give them new washing machine.
Boy: What have you got there to keep clean?

Refrain 4
Both: I like the shores of America,
      Comfort is yours in America.
      Knobs on the doors in America,
      Wall to wall floors in America!

Verse 4
Girl: I'll bring a T. V. to San Juan,
Boy: If there's a current to turn on.
Girl: Ev'ryone there will give big cheer.
Boy: Ev'ryone there will have moved here!

Refrain 5
Both: I like to be in America,
      Okay by me in America.
      Ev'rything free in America,
      For a small fee in America!